Communities

Living on an Island

By Joanne Winne

WITHDRAWN

Welcome Books

Children's Press
A Division of Grolier Publishing
New York / London / Hong Kong / Sydney
Danbury, Connecticut

Photo Credits: Cover, p. 5, 7, 9, 11, 13, 15, 17, 19, 21 © National Geographic Image Collection
Contributing Editor: Jennifer Ceaser
Book Design: Nelson Sa

Library of Congress Cataloging-in-Publication Data

Winne, Joanne.
   Living on an island / by Joanne Winne.
     p. cm. – (Communities)
   Includes bibliographical references and index.
   Summary: Three children living in Iceland, Madagascar, and Fiji describe what it is like
to live on their respective islands.
   ISBN 0-516-23305-X (lib. bdg.) – ISBN 0-516-23505-2 (pbk.)
   1. Island people—Juvenile literature. 2. Human geography—Juvenile literature. [1.
Island people. 2. Islands. 3. Island ecology. 4. Ecology.] I. Title. II. Series.

GN391.W56 2000
307.7—dc21

                                                                              00-023361

Contents

My name is Pétur (**pay**-tur).

Iceland is my home.

Iceland is an **island** with ice and snow.

5

This is the **village** where I live.

It is built along a **fjord** (**fyord**).

A fjord is an area of the sea between mountains.

I have two brothers.

My brothers and I like to sled.

We sled down the **snowy** hills.

My name is Hasani
(ha-**san**-ee).

Madagascar (**mad**-ah-gas-
kar) is my home.

Madagascar is an island
near Africa.

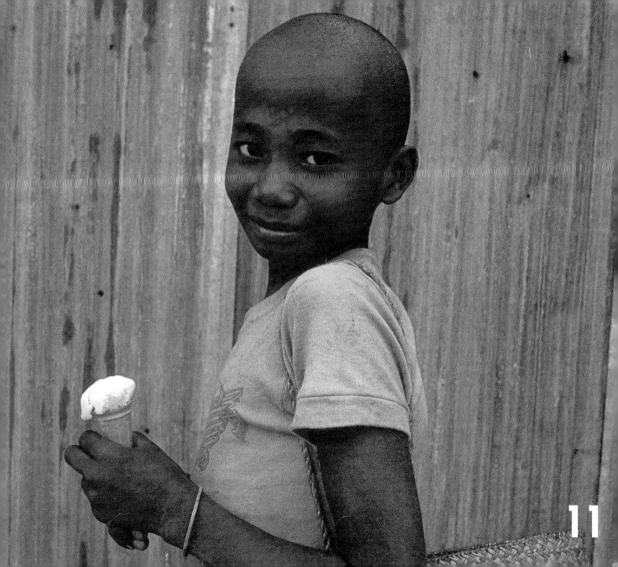
11

This is my house.

My house is made of clay.

It has a grass roof.

13

My father and uncle are fishermen.

They fish in the ocean.

They take the fish to the **market** to sell.

My name is Laila (**lay**-la).

Fiji (**fee**-jee) is my home.

Fiji is made up of many small islands.

This is my house.

The roof is made from dried leaves.

The leaves come from **palm trees**.

19

This is my mother and my little sister.

My mother is a **weaver**.

She likes making **colorful** rugs.

New Words

colorful (**kuh**-ler-ful) made of many
   different colors
fjord (**fyord**) a bay bordered by mountains
island (**i**-lend) land that is surrounded by
   water
market (**mar**-ket) a place where people
   buy and sell food
palm trees (**palm treez**) tall trees with no
   branches and many large leaves
snowy (**snoh**-ee) covered with snow
village (**vil**-ij) a group of houses, a small
   town
weaver (**wee**-ver) someone who makes
   rugs using pieces of yarn or cloth